A King's Guide:

31 Days to Choosing

a Proverbs 31 Wife

Pastor D. L. Williams

Printed in the United States of America
First Printing: October 2023
ISBN- 978-1-732-3942-5-4

Table of Contents

Dedication

To my beloved sons, Deshaun, Harrison, and Langston,

This guide is dedicated to you—three kings in your own right. As you each walk the path toward one day finding a wife with whom to share your lives with, may this collection of wisdom and insight from Proverbs serve as a compass to guide your heart, mind and soul.

It is my deepest hope that the insights within these pages inspire you to choose wives who will not only enrich your lives, bring you the ultimate happiness, but also contribute to the enduring legacy of our family. May you find women of virtue who bring richness, love, stability, faith, and the fullness of God's grace into our family circle. There is a Proverbs 31 Wife for you all!

As you make these significant choices of who to honor to become your wives, and represent your family's name, know that my heart swells with pride at the thought of the extraordinary young men you have become and will continue to develop into. Know that I am always so proud of you all. May your journeys be blessed with discernment and joy; and may you each create a home that reflects not *only the love you have seen in my marriage to my Proverbs 31 wife, but that echoes the love and teachings that have bound our family together through the years.*

With all my love and the highest hopes for your happiness and fulfillment,

Your loving father

Preface

Welcome, to a journey of discovery and discernment—a path that winds through the timeless wisdom of the Book of Proverbs. This devotional, **A King's Guide**: *31 Days to Choosing a Proverbs 31 Wife,* was born from a heartfelt conversation with my oldest son, who at 28 years old, vulnerably shared his readiness to embrace the responsibilities of being a husband, having a wife, and raising a family. Hearing him express these thoughts made me incredibly proud and affirmed that he, my "Young King," as I have affectionately called him since birth, was stepping into the next significant phase of manhood.

Moved by his genuine interest in this pivotal season of his life, I advised him to pray and fast through the book of Proverbs for the next 31 days. I suggested that he read a chapter a day, allowing the rich wisdom found within to guide his contemplations on relationships and marriage. However, after our conversation, I felt a strong prompting from the Holy Spirit to join him on this journey, to be his guide, and to share with him the insights revealed to me each day.

This book, in which you are now reading, is the fruit of that 31-day journey we embarked on together. It captures the personal insights I shared with my son and, by extension, his friends whom he shared them with in real time, as we delved deep into the virtues and challenges outlined in Proverbs. Encouraged by my wife, I decided to transform these fatherly counsels into a devotional guide to reach more young men like my son—those who might not have had the privilege of having such conversations with their fathers, or some other father figure.

Each day, as we progress from Proverbs 1 to Proverbs 31, the devotional will offer a specific scripture, a reflection on its implications for your personal growth and relationship choices, and a prayer to help cement these concepts in your daily walk with God. The goal is for you to not only read these words, but to reflect on them, pray them into your heart, and incorporate them into your life and your decisions.

This book is for those who are ready to seriously consider the role of a husband, not just in the worldly sense, but in the spiritual sense as well. It is for men who are prepared to lead with wisdom, provide with strength, and love with the heart of God Himself. Whether you are single, dating, or engaged, these insights will sharpen your understanding of what it means to find and cherish a wife of noble character. I even recommend all men pray through this devotional journey before proposing; to give Lady Wisdom an opportunity to speak to your heart and mind prior to you taking that leap into that next dimension of manhood.

So, open your heart to the wisdom of the ages, sharpen your discernment, and let's embark on this 31-day voyage together. By the end, you will not only be closer to finding the woman who will walk beside you in life or knowing what to look for verses what to run from, but also you will be more attuned to the spiritual call to be the man God has designed you to be for that special someone you choose to love covenantly before God.

I AM A MAN

by D.L.Williams

I am a man

I am

I am the crown of God's creation

created to be King

created to have dominion

created to build with a woman

I am

I am the priest of my home

protector of my village

provider of my family

a praying man

I am

I have a MAN-date on my life

I MAN-euver with wisdom

I MAN-ifest my dreams

I am MAN-DATORY

I am a man

Day 1: The Promise of Proverbs

Scripture:

Proverbs 1:3,5,33 "To receive instruction in wise behavior, righteousness, justice, and integrity." V5 "A wise man will hear and increase in learning, and a man of understanding will acquire wise counsel." V33 "But he who listens to me shall live securely and will be at ease from the dread of evil."

Devotional:

My Dear Brother,

As you embark on this 31-day devotional journey through the book of Proverbs in search for the clarity & insight you need in order to know what you should be looking for in a wife, as well as to seek understanding concerning the kind of man you need to become to be a strong husband— I want you to embrace the wisdom that these scriptures are geared to offer you. Proverbs is more than just ancient biblical text; it is a guide to living a life filled with righteousness, justice, and integrity. It is designed to shape your behavior, your mindset, and to sharpen your understanding. All the things you need to be a godly husband, and to know what to look for in a godly wife.

Even if you already consider yourself wise, Proverbs promises that you will gain even more wisdom and understanding by listening and learning. So do not take this journey for granted. Because if you approach this with the right heart, and open yourself to its insights, Proverbs assures you that by seeking the wisdom it contains, you will not only grow intellectually, but also gain the counsel needed to navigate life and the critical decisions we all must make in life.

Most importantly, Proverbs promises that those who heed its wisdom will live securely and free from the dreaded consequences of foolish behavior and foolish decisions. A profound peace that only comes from consistently making wise choices and following godly counsel.

As you read each devotion that I have prepared for you, I want you to pray for wisdom, instruction, and understanding each day. Ask God to fulfill these promises that Proverbs promises to give you as you take them to heart. Let the words of Proverbs and the gems I share concerning them for the next 31 days, guide you toward the wise decisions you seek to soon make concerning your legacy and future, so you can claim the peace and security it promises to give.

Prayer:

Heavenly Father,

Guide me through this journey of discernment with the wisdom of Proverbs. Illuminate my path as I seek a partner who embodies the godly virtues You cherish. Help me to - also develop the qualities of a godly spouse, that together we may build a life that glorifies You.

Grant me the wisdom to recognize the right qualities in a potential spouse and the patience to wait for Your timing. Protect me from haste and misjudgment and strengthen my heart with Your peace and guidance.

Thank You for Your promise to lead and guide those who seek You. I place my trust in Your perfect plan, knowing You will provide all I need according to Your riches in glory.

In Jesus' name I pray, Amen.

Day 2: Choosing Wisely

Scripture:

Proverbs 2:16-19 "Wisdom will save you from a woman who commits adultery. It will save you from a sinful woman and her tempting words. She has left the man she married when she was young. She has broken the promise she made in front of God. Surely her house leads down to death. Her paths lead to the spirits of the dead. No one who goes to her comes back or reaches the paths of life."

Devotional:

Today's proverb offers a vital lesson about relationships. Wisdom is not just a guide for making sound decisions in life; it is also a protector against harmful and destructive relationships. The scripture warns of the dangers of engaging with a woman who is unfaithful and whose actions lead away from the path of true life, and instead towards ruin. You see, the truth is that there are some women out here who can destroy your life. And these are the type of women wisdom is warning you to avoid. Avoid them because they can damage your life to such a degree that there is no recovering from the damage they have done. You and/or your life will be forever destroyed.

They can destroy your trust, destroy your love, destroy your health, destroy your name, destroy your desire for a godly unified family. They can destroy you in ways you cannot even imagine.

And wisdom's role is to not only protect you from being hurt by the wrong kind of woman, its role is to also guide you toward the right kind of woman. Because if you can learn the type of women to avoid, you will better be able to perceive the kind of woman you want to attract. That's what happens when you seek wisdom— it shapes your character and your choices; leading you to a partner who values integrity, faithfulness, and the promises made in marriage before God.

Pray for wisdom to guard your heart and mind. Let it steer you away from relationships that are toxic and bring harm, and towards those that are healthy and bring life. Trust that as you seek God's wisdom, He will lead you to a woman who will walk with you in righteousness, justice, faithfulness and love.

Prayer:

Heavenly Father,

Today, I come before You asking that you teach me to discern wisely, to recognize the dangers of unfaithful companionship, and to avoid those who might lead me away from Your paths of righteousness.

Equip me with spiritual discernment to identify and avoid destructive relationships that threaten my well-being and spiritual growth. Instill in me the virtues of integrity and faithfulness, that I may seek a partner who not only cherishes these qualities but also strives to embody them.

Guide my heart and mind in Your wisdom. Protect me from harm and lead me towards relationships that are nurturing, righteous, and reflective of Your love. Help me to trust in Your guidance, believing that as I walk in Your wisdom, You will lead me to a life companion who will join me in a journey of mutual respect, love, and godly commitment.

In the name of Jesus I pray, Amen.

Day 3: Trusting God's Direction

Scripture:

Proverbs 3:5-6 "Trust in the Lord with all your heart. Do not depend on your own understanding. In all your ways obey him. Then he will make your paths straight."

Devotional:

Today's proverb offers a powerful reminder about the importance of trust. Trust in the Lord with all your heart, and do not rely solely on your own understanding. Life presents many choices and paths, and it's easy to lean on our desires and logic. But God's wisdom transcends our limited perspective.

Involve God in every decision you make, no matter how big or small. Let Him captivate your heart for who to date, for who to give your time to, and for who to separate yourself from. Obey His guidance. Trust Him, and He promises to make your paths straight if you do! Which means He will lead you in the right direction, towards the right person, ensuring that your steps align with His perfect plan, and with the perfect person for your life.

As you seek a wife and consider starting a family, trust God's direction above your own desires. He knows your heart and your needs better than anyone. And you have to trust Him with your needs over trusting yourself with your wants. By placing your full trust in Him and seeking His wisdom for a wife, you will find the right partner and make choices that lead to a fulfilling and godly life.

Prayer:

Heavenly Father,

I turn to You, seeking Your wisdom and guidance as I am on the path to finding a life partner. Your Word reminds me to trust in You with all my heart and not to depend solely on the way I presently understand things.

Lord, I ask that You help me to trust Your plan for my life, even when it contradicts my own desires. Brighten my path and direct my steps toward the person You have prepared for me, someone who will not only share my life, but also grow with me in faith and love.

Teach me to trust You wholeheartedly, knowing that when I do, You will guide me the right way. The way that is best for Your will for my life. Let this assurance calm my anxieties and replace my impatience with peaceful anticipation. Give me the wisdom to recognize the qualities in a partner that honor You and reflect true godliness.

I submit my desires and my future to You, trusting that Your timing and Your choices for me are perfect. Thank you for being a faithful guide and a loving Father.

In Jesus' name, I pray, Amen.

Day 4: The Importance of Your Path

Scripture:

Proverbs 4:26-27 "Think carefully about the paths that your feet walk on. Always choose the right ways. Don't turn to the right or left. Keep your feet from the path of evil."

Devotional:

Your path in life is vitally important. So important that every step you take, and every decision you make concerning your life and future, needs to be intellectually approached, and not approached with just your emotions. The bible says, "think carefully," about your steps, and not to just rely on feeling out the vibes. Why? Because vibes don't mean anything! Vibes can be deceptive. Everything that feels good to you isn't always good for you. So, it's essential to know the difference between what feels right to you, and what truly is right for you.

So, stay focused on the path that you and God have set for your life, and don't deviate from that course! Don't allow yourself to be distracted by anything or anyone to the left or the right. You have to be steadfast and disciplined in your pursuit for this next season of your life. Your future is counting on you to make careful deliberation of your present choices.

Remember, wisdom calls for you to be intentional and thoughtful with every step you take. Trust in God's guidance and stay committed to the path He has you on.

Prayer:

Heavenly Father,

As I take this journey, I seek Your steadfast presence to anchor my decisions. Teach me to approach each choice with thoughtful consideration, grounded not in short-lived emotions, but in the solid truth of Your Word.

Help me to discern carefully the paths laid before me, distinguishing between what merely feels good and what genuinely is good for me. Grant me the wisdom to avoid distractions that veer me off the course You have set for me.

I ask for discipline to remain steadfast in my commitments, to stay focused on the goals and plans we have crafted together. In moments of uncertainty or temptation, remind me of the promises of Your guidance, and strengthen my spirit to persevere with intentionality.

Lord, I trust in You to lead me not just towards what is easy, but towards what is right and honorable in Your sight.

May my choices reflect my dedication to You and propel me towards a future filled with Your blessings and grace. In Jesus' name I pray, Amen.

Day 5: A Father's Hope

Scripture:

Proverbs 5:18 "May your fountain be blessed. May the wife you married when you were young make you happy."

Devotional:

My Brother,

In this verse from Proverbs, we find a father's heartfelt prayer for his son—to marry a woman who brings happiness and blessing into his life. This should be every father's desire for his son; for them to marry a young lady who adds emotional and spiritual value to his life.

Marriage is a sacred union ordained by our heavenly Father, that is meant to bring joy, companionship, and mutual support among believers. The choice of a spouse is one of the most significant decisions you will ever make. And you should seek a woman who not only shares your faith and values, but also who enriches your life in ways that bring you true happiness.

May God bless you with a wife who brings laughter to your days, strength to your challenges, and love that deepens with each passing year the two of you are together. As you continue this journey of seeking wisdom and praying for guidance, trust that God knows the desires of your heart and will lead you to the woman who is meant to walk beside you, and to help nurture a blessed life for the two of you. But know that if a woman is failing at making you happy with her spirit and personality in the dating phase, she will equally not succeed at bringing you happiness as your wife. You want a wife who has the endurance and the kind of temperament to make you happy throughout the duration of your marriage. A woman who can always make you happy instead of constantly making you miserable.

Prayer:

Dear Heavenly Father,

As expressed in the wisdom of Proverbs, I yearn for a partner who brings joy, not just in fleeting moments, but as a constant presence in my life.

Lord, guide me towards a woman whose spirit is kindled with Your love, whose personality echoes Your grace, and whose presence adds immeasurable happiness to my days. May she be a source of laughter, strength in challenging times, and a reservoir of love that deepens as the years unfold.

As I walk this path of discernment, help me to recognize the qualities that are enduring, those that will not only sustain but also enrich our lives together. I pray for a partner who shares my faith, and is committed to fostering a relationship that glorifies You in every aspect.

Grant me the patience to wait for Your timing, the wisdom to see clearly, and the heart to love deeply. May Your will be clear as You lead me to the one with whom I can build a life filled with blessings and mutual growth.

Father, I trust in You to lead me to a life companion who is not only my heart's desire, but also a manifestation of Your love.

In Jesus' name I pray, Amen.

Day 6: Choosing Wisely

Scripture:

Proverbs 6:25, 27-28 "Don't hunger in your heart after her beauty. Don't let her eyes capture you. You can't shovel fire into your lap without burning your clothes. You can't walk on hot coals without burning your feet."

Devotional:

Dear Brother,

Today's proverb is about sleeping with an adulterous woman, but its wisdom still applies to how to, and how not to choose a woman to be your wife.

First— beauty is significant, but it's still only surface. We all want a woman that's physically captivating— but some women who are flawless can also be fatal! Like a fire that can be enticing, but also destructive, some women, if not handled with wisdom and discernment, and with respect of the red flags they come with, can bring about a detrimental outcome that will be just as promising for you as is the outcome of playing with fire! Again, you will surely be burned!

What do you hunger for in a woman? Whatever it is— make sure it's something much deeper than her beauty and seductive ways. Hunger for things in a woman like an honesty, compassion, and the ability to be supportive. Look for someone with discretion, class, and grace. Someone who wants to be a mother or who has a mother's love within her. Someone who believes in prayer and who will pray for and with you. Feel free to add other such things to hunger for in a woman, but be wise enough to hunger for much more than beauty and seductive feminism. According to proverbs, pursuing beauty and seductive charm without considering other far more crucial aspects, can lead to pain and regret. Because those things alone don't always lead to a happy ending!

Prayer:

Lord,

Today's proverb reminds me of the dangers of superficial attractions and the deeper qualities necessary for a lasting and fulfilling relationship.

Help me see beyond external beauty and to discern the true nature of the women I encounter. Help me find a woman of honesty, compassion, supportiveness, and grace. May I be attracted to someone who embodies discretion and class, and whose life is rooted in prayer.

Guide my heart to desire more than just what my eyes see. Teach me to value and prioritize the virtues that sustain a marriage: faithfulness, kindness, and a shared commitment to You. Let me not be misled by charm or seduced by appearance, but rather be led by Your light to someone who will be a true partner in both life's joys and its trials.

Bless me with the patience to wait for the person who is not only captivating, but also capable of walking with me in faith, love, and mutual respect. May my decisions be guided by Your hand, trusting that You will lead me to a relationship that honors You and enriches my life in every way.

In the name of Jesus, I pray, Amen.

Day 7: Recognizing Red Flags

Scripture:

Proverbs 7:10-12 "A woman came out to meet him. She was dressed like a prostitute and had a clever plan. She was wild and pushy. She never stayed at home. Sometimes she's in the streets. Sometimes she's at other places. At every corner she waits."

Devotional:

Proverbs makes it so easy to tell what kind of woman to run from! If you take your time to digest its wisdom, it offers clear guidance on the types of women to avoid, and highlights specific traits that can lead to trouble and heartache. Recognizing these red flags is crucial in choosing a life partner wisely.

Here are the character traits of a woman to avoid, as described in Proverbs:

1. **Dresses provocatively**: She seeks attention through her appearance, often to lure men.
2. **Clever and manipulative**: She keeps a hidden agenda, usually aiming to secure a man with wealth or status.
3. **Wild and untamed**: She lacks domesticity and refuses to submit to a man, or to commit to one.

4. **Assertive and aggressive**: She pushes her own agenda and doesn't respect boundaries. She can't take no for an answer.

5. **Street-oriented**: She runs the streets! She loves being out and about rather than somewhere learning how to build a home.

6. **Constantly seeking**: She is always on the lookout for her next target.

Considering this, it is important to always study women and their traits. Consistent behavior reveals their true nature and whether they are worthy of your time and attention.

Seek a woman who values modesty, honesty, and a genuine relationship. Look for someone who is nurturing, supportive, and dedicated to building a family with you. True partnership is built on mutual respect, shared values, and a foundation of faith.

May you be discerning and wise in your choices, guided by the principles of Proverbs.

Prayer:

Prayer for Wisdom in Choosing a Life Partner

Dear Lord,

Grant me the clarity to recognize the red flags that Proverbs warns against. Help me to see beyond surface appearances and fleeting charms, to understand the true nature of those I meet. Teach me to value and seek qualities that contribute to a stable and loving home: modesty, honesty, commitment, and a nurturing spirit. May I find a partner who respects boundaries, shares my values, and is dedicated to building a life together under Your guidance.

Protect my heart from deception and my path from the pitfalls of unwise choices. Guide me away from women who dress provocatively to lure attention, who manipulate for personal gain, who resist commitment, and who defy the values You cherish.

Align my desires with Your divine wisdom for a companion who not only loves me but also honors You in all her actions.

Bless me with the wisdom to recognize the right partner, someone with whom I can grow in faith and love, and together, serve Your kingdom. May our relationship be a testament to Your grace and a reflection of Your love.

In Jesus' name I pray, Amen.

Day 8: The Power of Wisdom

Scripture:

Proverbs 8:14-16 "I have good sense and give good advice. I have understanding and power. By me kings rule. Leaders make laws that are fair. By me princes and nobles govern. It is by me that anyone rules on earth."

Devotional:

Dear Brother,

In this proverb, Wisdom speaks directly about her value and importance. And in speaking about herself, she lets it be known that she has something that you need— "good sense," and "good advice." Two things you need when choosing a future mate.

Wisdom also lets it be known that the most influential people value her because she helps them do what they do well. Kings, rulers, leaders, and royal nobles use her to lead effectively; to make decisions that strengthen their kingdoms. Which means to run your personal kingdom— you would be wise to use her too! As you seek out a wife for yourself, remember that choosing a wife is one of the most important decisions you can make. It's like a king selecting a queen to share his throne with. So, use the wisdom available to you to make a choice that will benefit you and the future you have left.

Prayer:

Father,

As I stand at the crossroads of decision, contemplating the future and the choices that will shape it, Your Word reminds me of the invaluable role wisdom plays not just in ruling kingdoms, but in every decision of our lives, including the choice of a life partner.

Lord, impart to me the "good sense" and bless me to hear "good advice" that wisdom and those with positive relationship experience have to offer me. As kings and leaders have relied on her guidance to lead nations, so too do I rely on her to guide my personal decisions. Help me to choose a partner wisely—a partner who will not only share my life but will also help to build and nurture our kingdom of love and faith.

Grant me the discernment to recognize qualities that align with Your virtues, and the courage to make decisions that are grounded in Your truth. May the choice of my spouse be thoughtful and enlightened by Your wisdom, so that together, we can build a life that reflects Your glory and love.

Help me to remember that in choosing a spouse, I am choosing a partner for life—a queen to stand by my side as we navigate the journey You have laid out for us. Guide my heart and my mind in this decision, and bless me with a relationship that exemplifies Your love and commitment.

In Jesus' name I pray, Amen.

Day 9: Leaving Childish Ways Behind

Scripture:

Proverbs 9:6 "Leave your childish ways and you will live. Walk in the way of understanding."

Devotional:

There comes a time in every man's life when he must grow up and leave his childish ways behind. To this point, you have grown up and left many things behind. Things like crawling, pampers, pacifiers, toy trucks, pouting...etc. Slowly, with each step you have taken, you have grown and moved closer and closer to manhood with everything you have left behind. Now, you are at the stage where it's time to leave another aspect of your past behind that will further evolve you into a man— being a ladies' man. Because chasing every woman who will allow you to chase her is childish! Any man can make himself available to as many women as he can. But it takes a real man to make himself available to only one woman, and to choose her to be the mother of his children. Just mentally being at this point in life is a big deal. And whoever you choose and whenever you choose her— it will be a pivot point of ultimate maturity and manhood. May God bless you for maturing to a place where you desire to be a one woman' man. This is a choice that if done with wisdom, will lead to a fruitful and fulfilling life for you.

Prayer:

Heavenly Father,

I acknowledge the journey of growth You have guided me through—from the innocence of childhood to the complexities of manhood. With each step forward, I have shed layers of my boyhood self to embrace the responsibilities You have set before me as a man.

Lord, as I endeavor to leave behind the ways of a ladies' man—to no longer chase fleeting affections but to earnestly prepare for a devoted and singular love, please show me the courage and the resolve needed to be a man who is available to one woman. The woman You have destined for me to cherish and respect as my partner and possibly even the mother of my children.

Guide me to recognize the right person, one who aligns with my values and Your divine principles. Help me to approach this decision with the maturity it warrants, knowing that such a commitment is not just a milestone of personal growth but a foundation for a godly and joyous future.

Thank you, Lord, for the grace that covers my past and the hope that illuminates my future. May my life and my love be a testament to the wisdom and maturity You continue to foster within me.

In Jesus' name I pray, Amen.

Day 10: A Father's Pride

Scripture:

Proverbs 10:1 "A wise son makes his father glad."

Devotional:

This timeless wisdom resonates deeply with me, especially when I think about my relationship with my oldest son. From his earliest days, he has always shown a remarkable ability to listen and trust the guidance I've offered. It's a trust that has been nurtured by my unwavering commitment to his well-being—ensuring he has the best opportunities in education, character development, friendships, financial stability, health, and reputation.

Every piece of advice, every correction, was delivered with his best interests at heart, aimed solely at his growth and success. Seeing him embrace these lessons, apply them diligently, and reap their benefits has been one of my greatest joys as a father. It's not just about obedience—it's about watching him internalize wisdom and let it guide his decisions and shape his life's course.

This is what your heavenly Father wants for you! To see wisdom doing for you just as she has promised. He wants to see you valuing wisdom and righteousness for yourself, and desiring to utilize it at every turn. He wants you to be a wise son, and to make Him glad in all you do. You will no doubt make your Father even more glad as you seek His wisdom to guide you to a woman to share your life with so to avoid making a regrettable mistake.

God's desire for you is clear: He wants you to be a wise son who makes Him glad by how you live your life, how you love others, and how you honor Him in all your choices. As you seek His wisdom to guide you in selecting a companion who aligns with His purposes, remember that this journey is not just about finding love but also about continuing to grow in wisdom, making decisions that reflect His teachings and bring glory to His name.

Prayer:

Heavenly Father,

I come before You with a heart full of gratitude for the gift of Your wisdom, the same wisdom that has guided generations before me. As I reflect on the relationship between a father and his son, and the joy it brings a father to see a child grow in wisdom and stature, I am reminded of Your paternal love for us, Your children.

Lord, You have placed before me the perfect example of wisdom through Your Word. Help me to cherish and apply this wisdom not just in small measures, but in all aspects of my life. Let it guide my decisions, shape my relationships, and influence my path.

As I seek a life partner, teach me to be a wise son, one who makes You glad by how I live, love, and honor You. May my life be a testament to the wisdom You have instilled in me, and may it inspire others to seek Your guidance in their lives.

May my actions and choices make You proud and bring joy to Your heart, as I strive to be a living example of Your love and wisdom.

In the precious name of Jesus I pray, Amen.

Day 11: The Value of a Kind Heart

Scripture:

Proverbs 11:16 "A woman who has a kind heart gains honor."

Devotional:

When seeking woman to build your life with, one essential quality you should look for in her, among other things, is if she has a kind heart. A kind heart goes a long way, and brings good things to those who possess it. And one of the good things that happens for a kind woman is that she gains honor. As a man looking for a wife, choosing her to be your wife is an honor that God has given you to bestow upon a woman. No woman can wear the honor of being a wife unless a man gives it to her. It is your honor to give as a man. It is a prize that God empowered you with. And if done right, it is an honor that you are to give once. Because after you give it— it's intended to be a decision you reap the benefits of for the rest of your life. Which means you cannot just honor any woman with the distinction of being a wife. This graciousness should only go to a special woman. It should go to a woman who among other things— is kind.

In the 24th chapter of Genesis, when Abraham sent his servant looking for a wife for Isaac, the main criteria used by the servant to distinguish the women was how kind they were. The woman who offered to water his camels set herself apart with her unusual kindness. That such a woman was worthy of the honor of being Isaac's wife. As you observe the women you meet, make sure that you are observing if the woman you find yourself most attracted to has a beautiful heart. That she's not just kind to the people you expect her to be kind to— but that she is kind to everyone and everything. Especially those she isn't expected to be kind to. Make sure she has a distinguishing kindness about herself. A kindness that sets her apart from other women. Because, among other things, a woman who has a heart of kindness like this is a woman who is worthy of the honor of being your wife!

Prayer:

God,

Please lead me to a woman whose heart reflects the kind of divine kindness that You value. In the search for a companion, help me to prioritize kindness and gentleness— traits that embody the spirit of Your love.

Grant me the discernment to recognize true kindness in action, and not just in words. May I find a partner who shows compassion and care not just to those from whom she expects a return, but to all Your creation. Let her kindness set her apart, making her a lighthouse of Your love and grace.

Bless me with the wisdom to understand that bestowing the honor of marriage is a sacred act, one that You have empowered me to give with great consideration.

As I observe and interact with those around me, instill in me a spirit of patience and a keen eye for genuine qualities. In Jesus' name, Amen.

Day 12: The Crown of an Excellent Wife

Scripture:

Proverbs 12:4 "An excellent woman is her husband's crown. But a wife who brings shame is like sickness in his bones."

Devotional:

Dear Brother,

The last proverb highlighted the honor that a woman with a kind heart gains. Particularly the honor of becoming a man's wife. Which also comes with the honor of becoming a mother and giving a man children— especially sons. But in marriage, the woman isn't the only person who should be walking around with some honor. The husband should also gain honor from his wife. According to wisdom, a man gains honor from his wife when she is the kind of woman who operates in excellency! Not perfection, but excellency.

Being a woman of excellency means she has a good character, she has integrity, she is a person of morals and ethics, she is a nurturer, she seriously values her relationship with God, and her growth as a Believer. Such a woman actively and intentionally works to grow as a person, a mother, and a wife. This type of woman brings honor to you as a man and husband. Because a woman of contrast can't give you such honor. A woman who behaves and conducts herself in a way that is shameful and embarrassing to you is like a cancer; bringing harm and distress to you. To avoid this, you must choose a woman a woman of excellency who will bring you honor, pride, and respect. A woman who makes you proud to be her husband; a woman who causes people to respect and value you more because she's your wife. So seek a partner who enriches your life, and enhances your reputation through the excellency she carries herself with. A woman capable of bringing you honor and not shame.

Prayer:

Lord,

Instill in me the discernment to recognize a woman of excellency. A woman who embodies integrity, and moral strength. Help me, Lord, to be a man worthy of such a woman. May I also bring her honor in the way I live, the way I treat her, and in my commitment to our union. Let our relationship be a testament to Your design for marriage, where both husband and wife bring out the honor and dignity in one another.

I pray that my future wife and I will uphold the values of excellency and honor, creating a foundation that will withstand the tests of time, and that will be glory to you as our maker.

In Jesus' name, Amen.

Day 13: The Deep Desire for True Love

Scripture:

Proverbs 13:12 "Hope that is put off makes one sick at heart. But a desire that is met is like a tree of life."

Devotional:

It's hard being in a place where you want something so badly that not having it makes you sick, especially when that something is love! When you find the one you desire so deeply that being without her makes you lovesick! It's a powerful sign of true love. There is nothing like the feeling of being in love, and loving someone so badly that you just feel sick without them.

The truth is— not everyone gets to experience this feeling. Not everyone experiences deep passionate love. Some settle, some are brought together by circumstances, and some are just after other things like security. It's rare to get that feeling when you love someone so deeply— not being able to have them the way you desire to have them makes you sick.

I hope you experience this blessing of being in love. I pray you find a woman that you crave, and who equally craves for you. A woman who you desire to protect with your life and to provide for even in your death. When you find this love, may it be like a tree of life for you, bringing you fulfillment and growth. This love, deeply rooted and nourishing, will be a testament to the strength and purity of your relationship. May you find it and forever cherish it when you get it. Choosing every day to never let it go!

Prayer:

Heavenly Father,

As I navigate the journey of life, I seek not just companionship, but a love that resonates with the kind of passion and depth that can only be sustained by Your grace. Lord, guide my heart to find a love so profound that its absence feels like a void, yet its presence is like a tree of life—nourishing, strengthening, and enriching. Grant me the blessing of finding someone with whom I share a deep and mutual craving, a partner who inspires me to offer protection, provision, and affection unconditionally for her.

I pray for a relationship that transcends the superficial, one that is rooted in genuine affection and mutual respect. May this love be a reflection of Your own steadfast love for us, marked by its ability to endure, flourish, and inspire.

Help me to recognize this love, and give me the strength to nurture it diligently, cherishing and honoring it as a precious gift from You. May this profound love not only fulfill my heart's deepest desires, but also glorify You in its expression and commitment.

In the name of Jesus I pray, Amen.

Day 14: The Skills of a Wise Woman

Scripture:

Proverbs 14:1 "A wise woman builds her house. But a foolish woman tears hers down with her own hands."

Devotional:

Being a wife is more than about a woman having a shape, looking good, or even being able to cook a good meal. Being a wife is about having the skills to build a family. According to proverbs, women have the power to build a loving family, or to tear it down. Which means there are only two kinds of women: constructive and destructive.

To be a constructive woman takes skills—skills like nurturing, organization, communication, diligence, prudence (forward thinking), submission, wisdom, and positive energy. In contrast, a destructive woman lacks these skills, exhibiting instead foolishness, negligence, laziness, poor judgement, lack of emotional regulation, and negative or toxic energy. With such she destroys her home! And you do not want a woman who destroys a home.

You would never go to a barber who hasn't shown the skills to cut hair, a mechanic without the necessary skills to work on cars, a plumber with no skills to fix pipes. No, you want the person with the skillset! Likewise, don't give a woman with no proven domestic, social, spiritual or emotional skills the position of wife is she hasn't demonstrated convincing skills to build a house. Look for a woman who demonstrates the skills to build a loving, healthy, Christian home. Qualities that will help her to build a strong and lasting family with you!

Prayer:

Heavenly Father,

Your Word clearly illustrates the profound impact a wife has on her home—she can either build it with love and grace, or tear it down with neglect and strife.

Lord, I ask You to lead me to a woman whose life reflects the qualities of a constructive partner. Grant me the discernment to recognize nurturing, organization, effective communication, diligence, prudence, submission to Your will, wisdom, and positive energy—traits that contribute to a flourishing home.

Help me to focus on the deeper, more enduring qualities that are necessary for a healthy, Christian marriage. Teach me to value a woman's spiritual and emotional skills as much as her domestic capabilities. May I find a partner who not only loves me, but also sincerely seeks to serve and honor You in our shared life.

Develop in both of us the desire to build a family that stands strong in the face of challenges, a family that grows in faith and love under Your guidance. Let us be partners who encourage each other in our walks with You, who manage our home as a testament to Your grace and who raise our children to know and love You.

Thank You for the wisdom You provide through Your Word, which guides us in our choices.

In Jesus' name I pray, Amen.

Day 15: The Importance of Love

Scripture:

Proverbs 15:17 "Better is a dish of vegetables where love is, than a fattened ox served with hatred."

Devotional:

Dear Brother,

If you don't have love, even when it seems you have everything, you really don't have anything! That's how important love is. So important, that if you have it without much of anything else, you really have all you need. Love, even with little else, makes you feel like you have it all! But much of everything without love is like having nothing at all. So, make sure you have love in your relationship. Love is the principal thing!

A loving relationship, no matter how modest, brings true contentment and fulfillment. Prioritize love in your life and seek a wife who values it and who is willing and able to reciprocate it back to you. This foundation will sustain you through all the trying circumstances that will no doubt come to test your love for one another.

Prayer:

My Creator God & King,

You have taught us that love stands supreme, transcending all worldly possessions. That without love, even the greatest treasures feel empty.

Lord, I seek Your guidance to find a soul mate who understands and cherishes the profound importance of love. Grant me the wisdom to prioritize this divine affection above all, recognizing that a life filled with love is rich beyond measure.

Help me to find a woman whose heart aligns with mine in the pursuit of true, selfless love—the kind of love that is patient, kind, and enduring. Let our relationship be a testament to the strength that love imparts, capable of weathering any storm and thriving in any circumstance.

Grant us both with a capacity for deep love that seeks the best for each other, that forgives without hesitation, and grows stronger through trials. May our love reflect Your love for us, unconditional and everlasting.

As we build our life together, let our love be the cornerstone that holds us steady and true. With love as our foundation, let us create a home filled with joy, respect, and understanding, a sanctuary where Your spirit dwells.

Thank You, Father, for the gift of love, and your example of what true love is.

In the name of Jesus I pray, Amen.

Day 16: God's Final Say

Scripture:

Proverbs 16:1 "The plans of the heart belong to man, But the answer of the tongue is from the Lord."

Devotional:

Your plans for your life are just that—"your plans." God gives us the freedom to plan out our lives. To plan our careers, to plan our financial life, to plan where we will live, to plan our marriages and who we will spend the rest of our lives with. You have the freedom to make plans for your future.

However, we must be spiritually wise enough to know and accept the fact that though God gives us the freedom to make plans for ourselves, He still has the final say. He has to say yes to our plans! And thank God for this truth; because who wants to make plans that are outside of God's will for us?

Yes, make your plans for who you will date, be in a relationship with, or start a family with, but still leave room for God to answer yes to your plans! Matter of fact, leave enough room for Him to even say no, b/c that's an option as well! Because if what you plan isn't what He has in His will for you, you want that no! I won't lie, no hurts sometimes. Especially when you were really passionate about your plan. But God's no can save you a lot of heartache and pain from things God doesn't have in his will for you. And when that's the case, you have to be mature enough to trust His no as much as you trust His yes!

Whatever His answer to your plan is, His answer is necessary to keep you in His will for your life. Which means when you plan, also pray! Plan for you a wife, and pray for you a wife! Plan so you can be prepared for what you desire, but pray so that you can know if what you desire is God's desire as well.

Entertain your desires, but don't forget to trust God's direction! And know that however He answers, His answer is always ultimately for your good!

Prayer:

God,

I acknowledge that while I may set my course, it is You who establishes my steps. You have blessed me with the freedom to dream, to plan, and to aspire towards various goals in life, including finding a spouse with whom I can build a life.

And as I freely make these plans, I submit them to Your sovereign will. Teach me to plan with wisdom and to pray with a heart open to Your guidance. May I always leave room for Your 'yes' or 'no,' understanding that Your decisions are infused with divine foresight and love, aimed at my ultimate good.

Help me to trust You completely, even when Your answers differ from my desires. If You say 'no,' give me the strength to accept it with grace, trusting that You are protecting me from potential heartache. If You say 'yes,' help me to proceed with gratitude and humility, always aware of Your hand in the blessings I receive. Today, I rest in the assurance that Your plans are better than mine. Therefore, I only want what You want for me.

In Jesus' name I pray, Amen.

Day 17: The Crown of Grandchildren

Scripture:

Proverbs 17:6 "Grandchildren are the crown of old men, And the glory of sons is their fathers."

Devotional:

Every man of value dreams of his bloodline. He dreams of it because he understands that his bloodline is his legacy. And every man of value desires to see his legacy come alive. Something that happens when his child gives birth to the next generation.

When a father gets to see his bloodline extend, his grandchildren become his crown. Every father gets to the age where he realizes that life is short. This is when he begins to value things that are truly important. Things like his legacy.

This proverb shows the wisdom of generational bonds. That fathers and sons must be bonded so that fathers can enjoy a natural bond to their grandchildren, allowing all to enjoy the joy of in the strength of the legacy they are all uniquely apart of.

Always value keeping the family bonds strong so that when you extend the legacy in which you are a part of, your son/daughter(s) will benefit from the strength of your family bonds. This will create a tight legacy of love, family unity and family values that will keep your children safe and surrounded by the things that matter most.

Prayer:

Dear God,

Thank You for the gift of family and the sacred bond that connects each generation in my bloodline. As I reflect on the importance of my bloodline and the legacy I wish to leave, I am reminded of the profound responsibility You have entrusted to fathers and sons.

Lord, I pray for the strength and wisdom to foster and maintain strong family ties not only with my parents, but all of my family where possible. Give me the strength to mend family relationships that have been broken. Help me to build a legacy that is not only marked by success and achievements, but that is deeply rooted in love, unity, and godly values. May my life serve as a foundation upon which future generations can build, grow, and thrive from.

Grant me the joy of seeing my children and grandchildren carry forward the principles and faith that have guided my journey. Help me to be a role model, a mentor, and a source of stability for my family, so that through my actions and teachings, they might see Your love and grace reflected.

May the legacy I contribute be one of righteousness, fostering a family lineage that honors You and upholds Your commandments.

Bless my descendants with the courage to uphold and continue this legacy that I am extending and building. May our family be a testament to the enduring power of Your love, and may our bonds remain unbroken across the generations.

In Your holy name I pray, Amen.

Day 18: The Blessing of a Good Wife

Scripture:

Proverbs 18:22 "He who finds a wife finds a good thing and obtains favor from the Lord."

Devotional:

As of 2024 there are 8.1 billion people in the world. And approximately 4 billion of them are women. Of those, about 1.5 billion of them are unmarried.

This sounds like you have a lot of options, right? Wrong! Alot of other factors will quickly dwindle that number to a meager figure. Factors such as attraction, geographical location, language spoken, domestic skills or non-skills, values/non-values, character, faith beliefs or non-beliefs, attitude, age, personality, mindset, diet, discipline, sexual history indicated by the number children birthed, chemistry, class, morals/ethics, communication skills, health (i.e. can she have children) and family structure.

Throw all of these in the mix, and those 1.5 billion women become a choice of just a few. Not every woman is wife material. All these factors combine to determine if a woman is wife material or not. To find a woman who is satisfactory in all, if not most of these areas mentioned above, means you have to hunt for her! You have to find her. Women who are wife material are not standing on every corner. They are gems, treasures, precious assets that must be found.

You have to be able to distinguish her among the other female distractions who are not wife material. When you are on the hunt for a wife, your focus must be laser sharp. Only looking for wife material.

Wisdom teaches men ready to be husbands, that it is wise to be on this hunt. Because when you find her, a true wife, you will have found yourself something real good; a good thing. The good thing isn't just the wife herself, but the good thing will be what you create with her once you make her your wife. Only a wife can produce a good thing with you. Other women can only offer you a good time. But we aren't after good times in this season. Good times fade and are only temporary. However, a good thing becomes legacy, and it last forever, because God will bless and favor your good thing, not your good times.

So Happy hunting! I pray you find a wife you can build a good thing with!

Prayer:

Father,

In a world abundant with choices yet complex in its diversity, I need Your guidance and wisdom. Help me, Lord, to not be overwhelmed by so many options, but to focus on the qualities that matter most. Grant me patience and clarity as I navigate the multitude of factors from character and values to compatibility and life goals.

Lead me to a woman who is a true companion in the journey of life—a woman whose presence enriches my life and whose spirit complements mine. Help me to recognize a woman of substance, a gem among stones, who will be a loving wife, a nurturing mother, and a faithful steward of the blessings we will share.

May my journey in finding a wife be filled with discernment, guided by Your light and truth.

In Jesus' name I pray, Amen.

Day 19: The Gift of a Wise Wife

Scripture:

Proverbs 19:13-14 "A nagging wife is like dripping that never stops. ...... a wise wife is given by the Lord."

Devotional:

This wisdom highlights two kinds of wives: A nagging wife and a wise wife. One is annoying, the other is refreshing. One you don't want to live with, the other you don't want to live without. One always complains and criticizes about problems, the other is always a solution to a problem.

Dear Brother, you don't want a nagging wife. Don't invite such a woman into your life. All she will do is bother you and drive you to frustration! You want a wise wife, because all she will ever do is present herself as a gift from God, constantly enriching you and making you better!

You don't want to always be frustrated in your marriage, do you? No, you want to always be growing into a better man, a better person, a better father for your children. And only a wise wife can help you do that.

So, choose wisely!

Prayer:

Heavenly Father,

Grant me the insight to identify a partner who brings peace rather than strife into my life. Give me the wisdom to choose a wife who will be a blessing in my life, one who encourages my growth, enriches my spirit, and enhances my role as a father and leader in our home.

Father, I desire a relationship that is rooted in mutual respect and love, where both of us strive to build each other up, and not tear each other down. Lead me to a woman whose presence is a gift from You, a true partner who reflects Your grace and wisdom in her actions and words.

Help me to be attentive to Your voice and receptive to the guidance You provide through Your Word and the Holy Spirit. May my choice in a spouse be aligned with Your will, bringing joy and peace to my heart always.

In Jesus' name I pray, Amen.

Day 20: Discern the True Character

Scripture:

Proverbs 20:27 "The spirit of a person is the lamp of the Lord. It lights up what is deep down inside them."

Devotional:

Dear Brother,

The best way to discern who a person really is— is not through their social media, it's through their spirit! This is God's design. God gave every human being a spirit. And according to this proverb, their spirit is God's lamp. It's what illuminates the core of a person, and reveals the deepest part of who they are so it can be seen.

A person's spirit is not just for the benefit of the person, but more so for the benefit of those around that person. God gave people a spirit so that others wouldn't have to be in the dark about who they truly are.

A person's spirit shines a light on their values, principles, maturity, mindset and more. And if God put a lamp in people, we would be wise to utilize the lamp He gave them! Meaning— take time to get beyond the surface of a person, so you can get to the spirit of a person.

Once you see what's really in a person, govern yourself accordingly! Don't be in denial about what's truly there.

Don't ignore the depth of who people really are. Make the proper decisions and judgments based on what their spirit shows you. Don't be in the dark when it comes to who people really are. God gave a lamp for you to see them; so you can know what you're getting or what you're not getting with the people you invite into your life and legacy.

Prayer:

Dear Lord,

Teach me discernment! Teach me how to recognize people not by what is merely seen, but by the spirit You have given to each individual.

Grant me the wisdom to look beyond what people want me to see, so I can see what you want me to see—the real them! Illuminate the spirit of others with Your holy lamp, revealing the core values, principles, and maturity that define who they truly are.

Help me to see with spiritual eyes what is often hidden from physical sight. Let me not be swayed by outward appearances but be guided by the truth revealed through the spirit of the woman I find interesting and attractive.

Give me the courage to make decisions and judgments based on the true nature of a woman's spirit. Protect me from deception and denial, and empower me to act wisely in relationships, fostering connections that are genuine, edifying, and aligned with Your will.

In Jesus' name I pray, Amen.

Day 21: The Impact of Communication

Scripture:

Proverbs 21:9, 19 "It is better to live on a corner of a roof than to share a house with a nagging wife. It is better to live in a desert than to live with a nagging wife who loves to argue."

Devotional:

Dear Brother,

Once again, the wisdom given to us for the 3rd time is that a nagging wife is not the kind of wife you want to have. Pay attention that the Bible keeps reiterating this to us as men! Nagging gets on the most patient person's nerves. And a nagging wife— no husband stand! The best man would rather escape his own home than to remain in it with a woman who complains and picks with him about every little thing she can possibly find.

A woman who loves to argue is not an easy woman to love or to be in love with. You need a woman with healthy communication skills. A woman who can communicate her feelings without nagging you all the time if at all. A woman who respects your mental health, and your emotional tolerance, rather than to disrespect them. Trying to share a home with a woman who shows no value for your mental and emotional well-being is unbearable my friend!

So, make sure the woman who interest you does not have an immature way of communicating. Make sure she speaks to you with respect and love. A relationship built on respectful communication will flourish. But one filled with nagging, griping, arguing and complaining will only wither.

Prayer:

Lord Almighty,

Today I am reminded of the importance of serene and constructive communication within a relationship. Your scriptures guide us to avoid the pitfalls of discord and to seek harmony with a woman instead.

I pray for a woman whose words uplift me rather than undermine me; whose presence calms me rather than agitates me. I seek a relationship filled with grace and mutual respect, where every conversation strengthens our bond and enriches our love.

Bless me with the patience to seek out a woman who approaches disagreements with a spirit of resolution and respect. May she value my emotional well-being as I cherish hers, fostering a home where peace prevails and love flourishes.

Lead our hearts to communicate effectively and compassionately.

Thank You for guiding my path towards the perfect peace that comes from following the wisdom of your word.

In the sacred name of Jesus I pray, Amen.

Day 22: The Right Start for Future Generations

Scripture:

Proverbs 22:6 "Start children off on the right path. And even when they are old, they will not turn away from it."

Devotional:

Most times when we think about starting our children off on the right path, we think about putting them in the right neighborhoods, sending them to the right schools, involving them in the right extra-curricular activities etc. However, giving your child the right start begins way before their neighborhood, school, and extra-curricular activities. I always tell men that the best gift you can give your kids is a good mother! Thats how you start them on the right path; by making sure you choose a woman who is worthy to be their mother.

Give your children a terrible mother, and they are indeed off to a terrible start in life. Give them a great mother, and their path is already a winning one. So, in choosing a wife, think about your children! Will your children value this woman as their mother as much as you think you will value them as your wife? If you aren't sure, then such a woman is either not the woman for you, or the mother for your children— or she is not that 'yet'. Maybe she still needs time to mature for those roles, and you need to decide if you are willing to wait for her to mature into that woman.

Either way— take your time to choose a woman your children will be proud to call mom. This choice will start your children on the right path, and ensure they have a strong foundation for the rest of their lives.

Prayer:

Lord God,

As I consider the profound impact of parenthood and the foundational role a mother plays in her children's lives, please guide me in finding a partner who will not only be a good spouse, but also a wonderful mother to our future children.

Help me to not only see my own desires for a wife, but also the needs of the children we may one day raise. Show me a woman who can provide our children with a loving, stable, and enriching environment.

Grant me the insight to discern whether a potential partner is ready to embrace the joys and challenges of motherhood. Bless me with the courage to make decisions that prioritize the well-being and development of my future children. May the mother of my children be someone who inspires them, teaches them, and guides them in Your ways, setting them on a path toward a fruitful and God-honoring life.

In Your holy name, Amen.

Day 23: Respecting Personal Boundaries

Scripture:

Proverbs 23:10 "Don't move old boundary stones."

Devotional:

We all have personal boundaries. According to proverbs, these are what we can call "boundary stones." A boundary stone was a physical marker used to show a person's property line. They were used to maintain a person's property line to ensure a person's property was respected and preserved.

Personal boundaries are similar to boundary stones. Personal boundaries are limits and/or preferences we set for themselves within relationships and interactions to protect our well-being. They help define what behaviors are acceptable and unacceptable from others that we will or won't invite into a more intimate space with us. When it comes to relationships, we can also see these as deal breakers. Boundaries that when crossed, terminate the relationship or possibility of there ever being one.

Like boundary stones, personal boundaries and deal breakers are there for a reason. There to protect something you value, be it your mental peace, your family unit, your dreams, your image, reputation, spirituality etc. The book of wisdom advises that we should never move our boundaries. If you set them up, you set them up for a reason. You should allow them to protect whatever it is you set them up to protect and maintain for your benefit. So never move old boundaries! Respect and uphold them to ensure your well-being and the integrity of the kind of relationship you wish to have.

Prayer:

Lord,

Your Word teaches the value of setting boundaries and keeping them in place. Inspire me to establish and uphold my own personal boundaries to safeguard my well-being and the kind of relationship I wish to have.

Help me to clearly define my limits and preferences in relationships. Grant me the strength to maintain these boundaries firmly, not out of selfishness or pride, but to preserve my mental peace, spiritual integrity, and moral values.

Give me the strength to remove myself from women who fail to respect my boundaries and who do not meet my preferences. Teach me to communicate my boundaries with grace and conviction when I need to, ensuring that they are understood and valued by those around me.

Let these boundaries be a testament to my commitment to living a life that honors You and that reveals my desires for myself.

I pray for the courage to never compromise on what I know is right for me in exchange for temporary comforts or pleasures. Keep my resolve strong and my path clear.

In the name of Jesus, Amen.

Day 24: The Value of Honesty

Scripture:

Proverbs 24:26 "An honest answer is like a kiss on the lips."

Devotional:

I was watching a dating show one day when the lady looking for a date asked the panel of men the question, "Do you prefer honesty or loyalty?" I thought it was an interesting question. Some of the men answered honesty, some answered loyalty. Most men want an honest woman though. My opinion is that we as men must first learn to be honest with ourselves before desiring others to be honest to us.

What good is it to require others to be true to you when you fail at being true to yourself? Many brothers have ended up in horrible relationship with women simply because they failed to be true to themselves. They allowed a young lady to stick around romantically who they knew wasn't a good fit for what they wanted in a wife, and it ended tragically! Likewise, many brothers have missed out on a good thing simply because they failed to be honest with themselves! They knew that young lady was a good woman, and that she was the one, but playing games and wanting to do what single men do, they lost a great chance at a great romance, and another brother got her!

Now they are stalking her social media saying, "Man, I had a good one right there!"

Either way, you don't want to be like one of these brothers. And the only way to avoid being one of them, is by practicing being true to yourself! Don't force anything by moving boundary stones, and don't miss out on a good thing by failing to be honest with yourself and your situation. In the words of William Shakespeare, "To thine own self be true." If not— you will regret it!

Prayer:

Father in Heaven,

Let me be a man who is true to his own heart and convictions, so that I can rightly expect the same authenticity from others.

Grant me the clarity to see myself with honesty—to recognize my needs, desires, and the areas where I may falter. Help me to be introspective and accountable for my actions, ensuring that I do not compromise my integrity or mislead others in matters of the heart.

Strengthen me, Lord, to avoid the pitfalls of settling for less than what I truly want in a relationship or of pursuing fleeting desires that lead away from the path You have set for me. Empower me to walk away from relationships that are not conducive to my spiritual and personal growth.

As I strive to be honest with myself, I pray that my authenticity attracts a relationship filled with truth, love, and fidelity. Protect my heart from deceit, both external and self-inflicted, and lead me to a love that is pure, uplifting, and ordained by You. In Your name I pray, Amen.

Day 25: The Beauty of Perfect Timing

Scripture:

Proverbs 25:11 "The right ruling at the right time is like golden apples in silver jewelry."

Devotional:

The only thing more frustrating than making the wrong decision— is making the right decision at the wrong time! In other words, life isn't just about your decisions— it's also about your timing. According to this wisdom teaching, when your decision is right, and your timing is right, the result is as beautiful and majestic as a beautiful artistic design that golden apples inside of a silver bowl creates.

Now you may not appreciate the beauty of that color scheme of golden apples with silver in the backdrop, but according to artistic history, this was known as a beautiful combination that was admired and appreciated by many. This is exactly what the proverb is trying to get us to know about the value in combining good decisions with good timing. That it's something to be appreciated, because the result of this combination is a beautiful thing. You don't want to make the right decision to marry the right girl too early, and you don't want to make the right decision to marry the right girl too late. Neither do you want to make the right decision to marry but marry the wrong girl! Same with having children. You don't want to have them too soon or too late. Because you will miss out on all the majestic beauty that comes with the wisdom of doing it in the right season.

So, as you ponder on what's right for you, also give great consideration to your timing. Because if your timing is off, the results you are expecting may not be the results you end up with. You have to have the right balance of patience and courage to know when— so you can win!

Prayer:

Faithful Father,

Today I feel the need to pray for insight on how to synchronize my choices with Your perfect timing. Teach me the art of patience and the virtue of discernment so that my decisions reflect not only wisdom but also the right timing.

Help me to value the profound beauty in making the right choices at the right time—a harmony that brings joy and fulfillment.

Grant me the foresight to know when to act and when to wait. Let me not rush into commitments prematurely, nor delay them out of fear or hesitation. Show me the right moment that aligns with Your will, ensuring that my actions lead to outcomes that are both fulfilling and honoring to You.

Provide me the courage to act boldly when the moment is right and the peace to remain steadfast when more preparation is needed.

Bless my heart with the assurance that Your timing is faultless, and that following it is the surest path to success and satisfaction. Help me trust in Your schedule, knowing that You orchestrate the best outcomes from our lives' intertwined timelines.

In Jesus' name, Amen.

Day 26: The Danger of Reckless Choices

Scripture:

Proverbs 26:10 "Anyone who hires a foolish person or someone who is passing by is like a person who shoots arrows at just anybody."

Devotional:

What do you call a boss or manager who 'knowingly' hires an incompetent worker, or a complete stranger off the street? According to proverbs, you call him the exact same thing you would call a mass shooter—reckless!

To be reckless means to act without thinking about the consequences; showing a lack of caution or thoughtfulness. This is the same principle that applies to choosing a life partner. When a boss or manager hires a fool or a stranger, he is guilty of two things:

1. Ignoring character just to have someone to fill a void

2. Failing to go through the vetting process to see if the person is qualified for the role.

Similarly, when looking for a life partner, you are guilty of recklessness when you ignore the character that the person has clearly shown you, or fail to take the time to vet the person who interests you. You are exactly what the boss/manager and the mass shooter are, because you have chosen a partner without thinking about the costly consequences of such a crucial decision without a certain level of attentiveness and carefulness.

Pay attention to character, and do your due diligence. Don't be reckless! Go through the process of knowing if the person you are deciding to spend the rest of your life with is qualified for the position, and not some random selection you are making without intent and precision.

Prayer:

Mighty God,

As Proverbs warns against recklessness, help me, Lord, to value character above convenience, to look beyond immediate attractions and assess the deeper qualities of those I consider inviting into my life. Teach me to conduct this vetting process with the thoroughness of a wise manager, not rushing to fill a void, but patiently assessing compatibility, values, and spiritual commitment.

Provide me the wisdom to avoid reckless choices driven by loneliness or impatience, which could lead to heartache and regret. Inspire me to ask the right questions, to seek Your insights through prayer and reflection, and to listen carefully to the answers provided by both words and actions. May my decision-making process reflect my care and attention to detail, ensuring that the partner I choose is indeed a blessing and not a burden; that she is an asset to my life, as I intend to be to hers—and not a liability.

In Jesus' name I pray, Amen.

Day 27: The Discipline of True Contentment

Scripture:

Proverbs 27:20 "Death and the Grave are never satisfied. People's eyes are never satisfied either."

Devotional:

My Brother,

There comes a time when enough is enough! But for some reason, some things in life never get enough. In Proverbs 27, we see that 3 of those things that never get enough are death, the grave and people's eyes!

As a man, this will always be true for you. Your eyes will always see women that are attractive, beautiful and at times even very tempting— but you must get to a place as a man where you are able to look, yet not pursue; where you can see yet remain satisfied with who you have already chosen to honor with your love.

It takes a disciplined man to marry. Many men opt out of marriage simply because they just aren't disciplined men. One of the reasons some men can't marry is because their eyes are never satisfied. They chase after every nice-looking woman they see! No woman or number of women are ever enough. They are always chasing after the next attractive girl or the next sexually available girl they see. Their eyes are never satisfied. But to become a disciplined man, you must be able to see, yet not pursue, because you have committed to not only your wife, but also to remaining a disciplined man. Though the eyes are never satisfied, and will always notice other beautiful women, being disciplined means your heart is satisfied and content with the beautiful woman you have chosen, pursued, and have committed your all to. It means you have trained and committed yourself to follow your heart and not your eyes.

So don't go after a woman to be your wife just because she looks good, because then she will only be what satisfies your eyes for the moment. It will not be long before you find yourself seeing another woman you like and would like to try and get to know. Instead, go after the woman who, though your eyes remain unsatisfied— she makes your heart content. She motivates your discipline to not pursue everything your eyes see, but only what your heart is content with. Your eyes will see many of nice-looking women. But to be a Christian husband, a godly husband, a disciplined husband—your heart has to be satisfied with the one you've chosen to have and to hold for as long as you both shall live!

Prayer:

Heavenly Father,

In a world filled with fleeting temptations and endless distractions, Proverbs reminds us that while death, the grave, and our eyes are never satisfied, we are called to a higher standard of fidelity and devotion.

Lord, fortify my heart with untiring discipline, that I may truly see, yet not pursue everything I see. Help me to appreciate beauty without always coveting it; to acknowledge attraction without allowing it to sway my dedication to the person I desire to love. Instill in me a deep contentment with the loving relationship You have blessed me with, that no outside allure can shake.

Teach me to channel my desires towards nurturing and deepening the bond I share with my significant other.

May my eyes not wander from the path of righteousness you have laid before me. Help me to embody the qualities of a godly husband who not only resists temptation, but actively cultivates a love that is reflective of Your own steadfast love for us.

In moments of weakness, remind me of my commitment. Grant me the grace to persevere in this commitment, honoring You, myself, my partner, and my legacy.

Amen.

Day 28: Cultivating Your Relationship

Scripture:

Proverbs 28:19 "Those who work their land will have plenty of food. But those who chase dreams will be very poor."

Devotional:

My Brother,

This proverb echoes yesterday's teaching about the natural tendency to desire everything we see and find ourselves attracted to. Today's proverb takes it a little further, and places emphasis on another important discipline that we need as men when it comes to relationships. This proverb stresses the importance of not chasing everything you desire, but learning how to put energy into what you already have so you can get more of what it has to give.

That is to say, you have to learn as a man how to invest your time, emotions, attention and care into the one woman you have. You have to work at that relationship. Get better at communication, affection, romance, etc., and see that when you do this—that one relationship will always keep you satisfied, because the woman will always allow you to reap the fruit of what you have been nourishing in her. The proverb says when you work on your land, you will have plenty of food! It will give you more than what you need! The same is true for a good woman who you give your attention. She will reward you with all the love, happiness, respect, affection, and more that you need. But you can't be on the chase for other women you find desirable!

It's time to stop chasing every dream girl and nurture a one-woman relationship. See what your efforts of faithfully pouring your all into this one relationship get you. If done right— it should return plenty to you!

Prayer:

Lord of Love and Loyalty,

I come before You with a heart eager to cultivate the relationship You have entrusted to me. As today's proverb teaches, help me not to be swayed by fleeting desires but to focus my energy on the woman I already have a precious relationship with.

Guide me, Father, to invest my time, emotions, attention, and care wisely and generously into my partner. Teach me to enhance our communication, deepen our affection, and strengthen our bond. Let me be diligent in the garden of this relationship, tending to it with the love and commitment it deserves, knowing that such dedication will yield an abundance of love and happiness.

Encourage me to see the value in what I already have; to appreciate the woman You have placed in my life, and to recognize her as a blessing that continues to unfold. Help me to understand that by nourishing this relationship with integrity and love, we will both reap the fruits of loyalty, respect, and mutual affection.

Prevent my eyes from wandering, Lord, and anchor my heart to this woman. I commit this relationship to You, asking for Your continual guidance and blessing as we journey together.

In Jesus' name, Amen.

Day 29: The Value of Time and Wisdom

Scripture:

Proverbs 29:3 "A man who loves wisdom makes his father glad. But a man who spends time with prostitutes wastes his father's wealth."

Devotional:

This proverb on today warns against the foolery of wasting your time with loose women. Yes, I said a waste of time, because the proverb uses the word "waste". Though it says he wastes his father's wealth— notice, that's not what it says he spends! Look again— the proverb says he spends his 'time'!

Let me tell you something about time. Time is a non-renewable resource. It is given to us by God to achieve not only His will, but also our goals, and to produce something meaningful with our lives. It is a resource that does not replenish. Once you use it, it's gone!

And when you spend your most precious non-renewable resource that is given to you by God to produce something worth producing and to achieve goals — on loose women who simply consume men's time for fun— you have literally wasted 'your' time! The time God has given 'you' to achieve life goals. Think about it: how much time have you wasted on a bunch of sexually charged women? Women who are unqualified to be given the honor of being a wife? Women who just consume men's resources?

There is an old song I am reminded of called "Man Eater". The hook of the verse says, *"Oh-oh, here she comes Watch out, boy, she'll chew you up Oh-oh, here she comes She's a man-eater Oh-oh, here she comes Watch out, boy, she'll chew you up Oh-oh, here she comes She's a man-eater!"*

Brother, I'm telling you, refuse to waste your time with these man-eating women who just consume and waste your time. Your time is more valuable than anything. Don't waste it on man eating women! By doing so, all you are doing is wasting the wealth of our Father's wisdom. Ignoring the gems He has left in His word to guide you. Love God's wisdom! God wants to see the wealth of His wisdom enrich you because He love you and wants to see you happy and blessed.

Prayer:

Heavenly Father,

Thank You for my life. Thank you for the time you have blessed me to have. A precious resource that I realize cannot be reclaimed once spent. Teach me, Lord, to value this gift, using it not for shallow pursuits, but for fulfilling

Your will and enriching my life with meaningful relationships and endeavors.

Help me to steer clear of relationships with women that drain my resources and distract me. Help me to avoid the entanglements that empty me in so many ways. Give me the mindset to invest my time and love in someone who is worthy of the commitment of my time.

Protect me from wasting my time on women who do not honor You or line up with what I am looking for in a woman. Remind me daily of the value of each moment, urging me to spend each one with those who matter to me and where I am going with my life. May I walk in this wisdom, not deviating to the left or right, and may the choices I make with my time glorify You and bring joy to my heart.

In the mighty name of Jesus I pray, Amen.

Day 30: The Importance of Choosing a Worthy Wife

Scripture:

Proverbs 30:21-23 "There are three things that cause the earth to tremble. There are four things it can't stand: a servant who becomes king, a foolish person who eats too much, an unloved (contemptible) woman who gets married, and a female servant who takes the place of her female master."

Devotional:

As we are only one day away from bringing this journey to an end, Proverbs 30 makes a slight shift in the wisdom source. Up until now we have been widely blessed with the wisdom of Solomon and many of his wise sayings. But now we are given the wisdom of another wise man by the name of Agur. We are not sure who he is, but the wisdom he gives is insightful. In this proverb, Agur highlights threats to the social order and natural hierarchy of society that, for him, are unsettling. He highlights unsettling scenarios that come to disrupt social stability and the social norms which make our society collectively stable. Among these unsettling scenarios is the unsettling scenario of a mean and unqualified woman being made a wife.

According to Agur, men marrying women who are unqualified to be wives will cause a deterioration of our modern society like an earthquake does to the very foundations of the Earth. Basically, this proverb from Agur warns men against marrying women who clearly do not have the character to be a wife. His position is that putting women in such a honorable position in society will be the cause of human civilization to rot; because such women cause the family structure to be unhealthy, unproductive, contentious and unstable. And the natural effect of this will be an unhealthy, unproductive, contentious, and unstable community.

In other words, men not only do themselves a major disservice when they honor women to be wives who aren't qualified to be wives or mothers, but we do the entire community a disservice!

So, do yourself and society a favor— do not deviate from the normal social practice of elevating only women who are deserving, qualified, and fit to be wives. Consider it strongly inappropriate, unbecoming, and irresponsible for you to do so. Be responsible and help your-self and society out by choosing a woman who will add value to not only your life and the life of your children, but also— to the larger social order! Give the community another queen who will add value to modern day society just as she holds the capacity to add value to you!

Prayer:

Lord of Wisdom,

I am reminded of the profound impact that our choices in marriage have not only on our personal lives, but also on the fabric of society. Help me, God, to understand the weight of this decision. Enlighten my heart and mind. Let me be drawn to a woman whose character strengthens the bonds of family and community, and whose presence is uplifting.

Guide me to a partner who will be a queen in our home and a beacon of integrity in the world. I want to take seriously the responsibility to make this choice not just for my own happiness, but also for the betterment of all who will be touched by our union. May the woman I choose to honor as my wife be deserving of such a role, equipped by You to thrive in it and to help forge a legacy of faith, love, and stability.

In Jesus's name, Amen!

Day 31: The Price of a Proverbs 31 Wife

Scripture:

Proverbs 31:10 "A wife of noble character who can find? She is worth far more than rubies."

Devotional:

Well my Brother, here we are!

We have reached the final chapter of Proverbs. Where we find the wisdom of a King by the name of King Lemuel. The words of this king are most famous for introducing what is widely known as "The proverbs 31 woman," in which should rather be called, "The Proverbs 31 wife," because she isn't just a woman— she's a wife! This is the woman that we have been on the journey towards since you first started this journey on day one. Ironically, this is the woman you should be on a journey towards in real life.

The wisdom Lemuel shares in this proverb is not from his own original words, but rather from the wise words of his mother! Making Proverbs 31 words of a Queen mother to her young King son about how to act like a young King, and the kind of woman he should choose to be his Queen!

He says his mother taught him not to give the best years of his life over-indulging in relationships with a bunch of loose women. This is something we just mentioned on day

29 when we discussed wasting your time on women who are sexually charged and unqualified to be a wife. Instead, she advises him to find himself a worthy woman. A woman who she describes as to not being easy to find, because she asks the rhetorical question, "who can find her?" I think a better way to interpret this question may be, "who is the man that can win her?" I say this because she mentions the price of this woman being more than the price of rubies. Meaning that the man who lands this worthy woman must first be a worthy man; a man qualified for the value she this kind of woman brings; a man who has his stuff together; a man who has the price of her value in hand, because he *is* the price of her value!

Proverbs ends encouraging brothers that worthy women are out there! But that brothers must first do the necessary self-work to even be able to attract this caliber of woman. The essence of your life must be the price of her worth! You can't be a $35,000 caliber man in the market for a $150,000 luxury vehicle! You are in the wrong lot! To be in the market for a luxury caliber woman, you have to increase your value as a man. And Lemuel's mother makes it clear that the self-work a man does to increase his value to attract such a woman, is well worth the price that must be paid to land her. Well worth the work that must be invested to improve himself, and well worth the time and patience invested to find her! So, brother, keep working on yourself as you are in search of this Proverbs 31 Wife. Keep paying the price!

Taking care of your body and your health— that's the price! Changing your social circle and making it more positive— that's the price! Getting closer to God— that's the price! Becoming well read and expanding your mind— that's the price! Doing the work it takes to become a gentleman—that's the price! Becoming disciplined with the way you manage money— that's the price! Reserving yourself sexually— that's the price! Working on being a devoted and faithful man— that's the price!

You must do what is necessary to increase your value as a man if you want the kind of woman whose worth is more than rubies! This kind of woman is rare! She doesn't come a dime a dozen! She's not on every corner like a loose woman! She is special, hard to find, and isn't attracted to any brother! You can't be lazy and get this woman. You have to become the price! Because if and when you truly find her, you want to be everything she is looking for in a man. You have to be able to secure her. She needs to be able to see the tangible evidence that you are the kind of king that is fit for a worthy queen!

Prayer:

Lord God,

As I stand at the end of this journey through Proverbs, I am inspired by the teachings concerning the virtues of the Proverbs 31 woman—a standard not just for women, but a beacon of light guiding me towards becoming a better man.

Lord, empower me to undertake the necessary self-work to elevate my worth to match that of the virtuous woman I seek. Help me not to waste my best years, but to invest in becoming a man of substantial character and value.

Grow within me the discipline and the desire to do the work on myself so that I can be a man that reflects you. Let me be diligent in managing my resources wisely, preserving my integrity, and enhancing my capacity to love and lead a family.

God, as I strive to match the value of the Proverbs 31 wife, I pray that You mold me into a man worthy of such a partner. May my life reflect the richness of Your teachings, showing evidence of my readiness to meet, cherish, and honor a woman of such noble character.

Grant that my journey towards this goal not only prepares me to meet her, but also shapes me into the man I need to be for her. A man who contributes positively to the world and who can stand as a king beside a queen, equally yoked in Your service and love.

Thank you, Lord, for the vision of a life partnered with a woman of great virtue, and for the guidance to aspire to be her equal in worth. May my actions and choices bring me closer to this reality. In the name of Jesus I pray today, Amen.

Final Thoughts

As we close this journey through the Book of Proverbs, I hope that the daily reflections and prayers for the last 31 days have not only enriched your understanding, but also inspired you to actively pursue the kind of love and partnership that God desires for you. Each day, we've explored the wisdom that Solomon and other wise contributors laid out—a roadmap not just to any relationship, but to one that is deeply rooted in godly principles and mutual respect.

The gems we've uncovered are more than mere suggestions; they are foundational stones for building a life that is not only fulfilling, but also pleasing to God. From discerning the character of a potential spouse to fostering love and respect within a relationship, these principles are designed to guide you towards a domestic life that is both fruitful and prosperous.

As you move forward, I encourage you to hold these teachings close to your heart. Use them as a compass as you navigate the complexities of relationships. Remember, choosing a spouse is not just a decision for today—it's a decision that will shape your future and, should you be blessed with children, the future of the next generation.

A godly wife is a treasure more valuable than rubies, and the effort you put into finding her will be rewarded with joy and companionship that lasts a lifetime. Approach this pursuit with prayer, patience, and persistence, always seeking God's guidance above all.

As you harness these gems, I urge you to pass them on to your sons, brothers, and other men in your life who might benefit from sound, unbiased guidance on one of the most important decisions of their lives—building a life with a Proverbs 31 wife. Let this wisdom ripple through your conversations and interactions, enriching not just your own life but also the lives of those around you.

May you find a partner who not only shares your dreams, but also your devotion to God. Together, may you build a legacy of faith, love, and righteousness that will stand as a testament to the power of a life led by divine wisdom.

www.ingramcontent.com/pod-product-compliance
Lightning Source LLC
Chambersburg PA
CBHW071149090426
42736CB00012B/2285